THE GRAIN OF MY LIFE

POEMS

BY

MUIR HUNTER

1943-1997

TEARS IN THE FENCE

THE GRAIN OF MY LIFE

First Edition 1997

©1997 Muir Hunter QC

All Rights Reserved

ISBN 1 900020 12 2

Photographs © Gillian Petrie 1997

Published by:

Please re-order from:
Muir Hunter QC
P.O. Box 71
Shaftesbury
SP7 9RW
Cheques payable:
Muir Hunter Book Account

Printed by Hobbs the Printers Ltd, Totton, Hampshire SO40 3WX
from camera-ready copy supplied

FOR VICTORIA,

ALSO KNOWN AS GILLIAN,

THE SUBJECT OF SEVERAL OF THESE POEMS.

Illustrations:

The road is the A303

The iron sculpture:
The Man in the World by Gamundi
Caspe, Spain, c.1974

The marble sculpture:
a reproduction of
Discobolos
by Myron of Athens, c.431 BC

The trees portrayed
are Wiltshire trees

FOREWORD

Muir Hunter's work springs from a deep humanitarian concern, borne out of the terrors, horrors and moral disappointments that living in the twentieth century has engendered in many of us. There are poems here of war and of the war we wage against the natural world. These things are informed by an awareness of the witness of history. His classical background shines through, as does his important work for Amnesty International. For Muir Hunter, poetry is intensely relevant to our place in Time. He writes of things - sometimes uncomfortable truths - that matter, or should matter, to every one of us. And the way he writes gives hope to transcend the pain and suffering.

There are deeply tender poems too: about a garden gently worked "with mind and hand" (a good metaphor for the making of a poem itself), about the child who would become the man - and about love. These words have had their forming in many parts of the world. But we come home in the end to a beloved landscape, and the determination that it shall survive for our children's children. To care for such things, as to care for human rights and humane justice, is necessarily to take a stand. This book takes its stand on a firm rock, and that rock is love.

Sean Street
Poet and Broadcaster,
1997.

THE GRAIN OF MY LIFE: CONTENTS

*   *   *   *   *   *   *

TARMAC AND TEARS

The blood of the earth flows out like a river,
Down the motorway's tarmac bed.
Tar is black and blood is red,
Purple is the sheen on the scene of bloodshed,
Oil and petrol, copper and steel,
Granite and limestone, gold and silver;
And the tread of the tyre of every wheel
Hums:

    Tears on the tarmac, tarmac and tears.

Elements forged in the stars over aeons,
Diamonds cut by celestial spheres,
Atoms bejewelled with a myriad electrons,
Coal distilled by a million suns,
Frittered away in a span of years.
Glaring the headlights, lurid the neons,

    Tyres on the tarmac, tarmac and tears.

Where are we hurrying, devourers of nature,
Vampires sucking the elements dry,
Cannibals battening on our future,
Heedless of culture, thankless to nurture,
Every man his own bald vulture,
Rolling tarmac up to the sky?

    Tears on the tarmac, death on the way.

Arteries of oil gush, gold veins are leaching:
Is there no surgeon to staunch the gore?
Everywhere on Earth the dams are breaching,
In dried-up seas the ships are beaching,
No rich lode is too deep for reaching,
As the predators mine her innermost core.

    Tears on the tarmac, blood on the ore.

Tears of blood on the red-hot tarmac
Boil away as our brief lives pass.
Blood is red and tar is black,
Purple is the gleam on the river of glass.
Mix red and black for a purple pall,
Fit for a shroud for imperial Caesars,
Laurel-wreathed for a dead world's funeral,
Crowned at the end with a cosmic coronal.
Fierce are our fears lest our dear Earth's heart crack,
Give us our Garden of Eden back!

    Tears on the tarmac, tyres on the tarmac,
    Death from tarmac, tarmac and tears.

Wiltshire,
1989-1990.

ASHES OF EMPIRES: An Epitaph on Yugoslavia.

This land was ruled by Roman swords,
From towns laid out like chequerboards,
    And the flash and the clash
    Of the bronze cuirass
Kept at bay barbarian hordes.

Pannonia they called it then,
Breeder of fierce highland men,
    To whom blood and death
    Were as natural as breath,
And clan feuds smouldered in every glen.

Generals were born and burgeoned here,
Ruthless, bold, yet passing austere,
    And Emperors were bred
    By the soldiers they led,
For the throne of Rome was temptingly near.

Savage tides lap to the top of the Wall,
But ambitious generals care not at all,
    On a gambler's throw,
    The legions must go,
And the Goths pour through like a waterfall.

The fall of the West lets in the East,
Strange realms ruled by an emperor-priest;
    And the Orthodox rite
    Is the handmaid of might,
Greek Romans presiding over the feast.

The centuries pass and the Turks hold sway,
The crescent has driven the cross away,
    But the fierce highland men
    Fight from peak and from glen,
As the Turks tighten their yoke each day.

A spin of the wheel, and the Hapsburgs rule,
Sometimes a tyrant, sometimes a fool,
    Releasing that yoke
    Is an Austrian joke,
While the Great Powers fish in the Balkan pool.

But Nemesis waits for the Northern Rome,
With Hapsburg blood as the fuse of the bomb,
    When the shots from the gun
    Of Serbia's son,
Doom us all to the hecatomb.

The Powers conspire to jerrybuild,
A nation too long a battlefield,
    With crescent and with crucifix,
    In a mad match and mix
Of tribes who would rather die than yield.

These heaps of ashes of empires past,
Each more unstable than the last,
    Can be kicked into flame,
    By a frontier, a name,
Old feuds exploding with lethal blast.

Catholic, Muslim and Orthodox,
Three fierce faiths in a narrow box,
    And neighbours in town
    Are for shooting down,
On each door the executioner knocks.

How many Gods are there, one or three,
Each watching His son on the calvary tree?
    Pitiless winds make the bodies turn,
    And the ethnic cleansing fires to burn,
While the living cry: May my God save me!

Wiltshire,
May 1993.

The Army supplied the slabs, our slaves laid them,
Centurions surveyed it, laid out the road,
Just a light ford, for chariots and farm-carts.
It's lasted pretty well, though winter storms
Sometimes dislodge the stones, which the slaves put back.

My father sits in his tunic, grave, grey-bearded,
His general's scarlet mantle laid aside.
I see the scars like badges on his arms,
I have prodded the pit the Parthian arrow left
In his thigh. "I wince still," he jokes, "Remembering
The mess the sawbones made, digging it out.
A priestess used some magic herb to heal me".

I think of Pompeius, Caesar, Divine Augustus.
"Will our empire last for ever?" I ask.
"Nothing lasts for ever," he says. "In Parthia,
When I served there under Divine Trajan,
Our armies marched past many a ruined city,
As big as Londinium, maybe as big as Rome,
Now just bricks, bones, ashes, silted canals.
Merchants there told how the Land of Han,
Far to the east, built a wall against barbarians,
As long as the road that runs from here to Rome.
It still failed to stem the tribal hordes.
Our legions built such a wall for Hadrian Caesar,
To fence out savage Caledonian tribes.
How long will our wall keep out that fierce flood?
Walls are for scaling, fences for pulling down.
Remember the poem you read to me last winter:
'Fence not your frontiers, pacify men's hearts'."

Soon I must go to Rome, in my family's footsteps,
To learn the law and politics and war.
And how, like my ancestors, to govern men.
My father says that I must watch my back,
Watch, too, the strange new gods, and one called Christ,
But, most important, watch the Emperor's face:
His smiles, his frowns, will mark who's in, who's out.

THE FORD ON THE EVENLODE

.... In barbaricum mare frustra
Imperii aedificant moenia limitibus.

I, Muir: A.D. 1936

It was a hot summer's day; I was at Oxford.
My father had come on a rare visit to see me,
Grave yet merry, a learned man, unsuited
To the grey ambitious civil service life.
I owed him so much, so little yet repaid:
The riches of languages, history, archaeology,
All learned from him.

We picnicked by the river Evenlode,
His ancient car tucked into the spinney's shadow,
The river chuckling beneath us. He sat on the bank,
I stripped and splashed in the river, barely knee-deep,
Dragonflies darting around me, peacock-blue.
"There are a lot of flagstones here", I called,
"What can they be?" "A Roman ford, I'd guess,
The Roman road passes just north of here.
This would have served a villa. We'll look on the map.
The water would have run deeper then,
Before long axes felled our ancient woods."

I heaved at the Roman paving, a boy again
On a Sussex beach with Father, I built a weir.
The water level rose, the stream ran faster.
My mischievous thought: what will the fish do now?

II. Gaius: A.D.136

My father sits on the bank, above the river,
While I swim in its sunlit dancing waters,
Dragonflies darting around me, peacock-blue.
His chariot is safely hitched in the spinney's shadow,
A fast Army twin-horse, he let me drive.
This ford, he told me once, was built by his father,
In the good old days of Governor Agricola,
When his father got the land and began our villa.

5

I do not want to go to a Rome like that.
I'd rather swim underwater and watch the fish.
Should I pray to our river-god that I don't go,
But stay on here and manage our estates?
Fat chance of that!
                    A cloud covers the sun.
The chariot-horses stamp, their harness jingles.
"Time to come in, Gaius," my father calls.
"Venison for dinner, you'll try the wine again,
But mixed with water, as a boy should drink."

III. Muir to Gaius: A.D.1936

A cloud covered the sun. My father called,
"Time to be off, Muir, come out now and dress.
We'll look for supper in a pub nearby."
I gazed down at the weir I'd built so blithely,
"Don't worry, Gaius," I whispered, "it won't last.
The winter freshets will flatten it, freeing the fish.
Thanks for your ford, the splashing and the fun.
I ought to tell you: I am a Caledonian;
Your father's wall couldn't fence us out for long."

I had to go to my Rome, as he went to his,
To learn the law and politics and war
And how not to govern men like my ancestors,
Thinking of Gaius' ford on the Evenlode,
And the futility of fencing empires,
While the sun was setting on ours,

                    As it set on theirs.

Wiltshire,
July 1992.

7

BRICKMAKER BOY

A young boy, I, at the end of our garden,
Watching the men, deep-chested, sinew rich,
Working the clay.

Their silvery sweat shines through their vests:
Arms rise and fall, pounding the brick-mix,
Kneading the clay.

They dig the Sussex clay from the field about us:
The best in England for making bricks.
The sheet of clay

Covers the land from the downs to the sea.
The glaciers spread it here, finely-ground,
From the northern mountains,

Long since eroded. The clay runs into the sea;
The gentle slopes, ungroyned, we slither down
Are eaten hungrily by the breakers.

Clay, water, sand,
More sand in the forme to prevent it sticking:
Flouring a cake-tin.

The unformed ball of clay
Must make a brick of exact dimensions:
Eight by four, by two and a half,

The English size. The brick-makers
Throw me a lump to squeeze and play with;
They knead and beat, knead and beat,

A rhythm of kneading and beating.
Now the mix is right, elastic, malleable,
Into the forme it goes, sliced off with a knife.

No cranny or crevice is unfilled
The bricks in their formes are put out to dry,
Stacked, awaiting the fire.

Within the kilns, fed with Sussex charcoal,
Very hot and very slow, the bricks turn pink:
Pink Sussex bricks for Sussex houses.

To-day, there are no men, deep-chested,
Silvery-sweating, bashing the clay;
Just an gaping hole in the ground

Where clay was mixed with sand and water and fire,
Where clay cliffs ran down to the ungroyned beach,
When I was a brickmaker boy.

Wiltshire,
1995-1997.

DESERT JOURNEY

Our road was ever rugged through the desert,
Blinding heat by day, frost many a night.
My caravan had a hard row to hoe -
Not that any hoe could pierce that soil -
The going killingly hard on the hooves of our mounts,
Or treacherously soft on the dunes' deep breasts,
Where quicksands lay in wait with a sly slow death.
We ate well, hunting gazelle, swift, hard to hit,
Migrating, thirsty, seeking water like us,
Wild oryx, ibex, lynxes, prairie hares,
The occasional mountain lion, to be skinned, then eaten.
Sometimes we found in hollows melons or gourds
When the dates and figs were finished.

                    Deserts know
Little of peace, with hostile tribes, bandits,
Night marauders, to be battled with, beaten off,
Blood on our spears, the desert littered with bodies,
For myself, I used no venom on arrow barbs.
Some days, at vital wells, too strongly defended,
Hard-fought bargains played the role of battle,
Buying the water truce: "Fill your bags, strangers,
And begone!"

                    We often dreamed of water,
Mirages cozened us with rivers, lakes
And fountains - we could hear their basins' music -
Shams of the desert genie. All this we bore,
With many a wound to show, many unmarked graves
Lapped by the dunes, built round with cairns of stones,
Scant water we had to wash their butchered flesh,
Their blood-soaked tunics the only winding-sheets
We could afford. Can it be, we would ask one another,
That the mountains to-day were nearer than yesterday?
Or was that a mirage too?

                                        And then you came,
Born of the dune sands, dust-devil made flesh.
You joined my caravan, close-wrapped in your veils.
Only your eyes shone out, like the night's fierce stars.
You glided over rough ground as if it were marble,
And you a princess glimpsed between porphyry pillars,
Circled by cool breezes from a fountain's play:
Real fountains, we felt, and you a real princess.
You rode, ever tireless, on a milk-white mule,
Radiating calm, complaining of nothing,
Disclosing nothing about yourself, your tribe.

We soldiered on, heat worse, water-bags leaner.
The peaks began to pierce the pitiless sky,
But mist still veiled their grim anatomy,
Huge in the desert haze, bulk without form,
No hint as yet of their geography.
But one day the mist rolled back, and we were there,
At the foot of the mountains, steep, bleak precipices.
No way up could we see, and no way around.

The heat glared fiercely back at us from the rocks
All through that night. In the dewy desert dawn,
The morning's water-roster mocked at our thirsts.
No streams gushed from the mountains' grim facades,
No green patches hinted at damp beneath.
This, then, was the end of the road: our place of death.

You stood apart from our huddled, desperate councils,
Wrapped, as ever, in veils, gaze calmly fixed
On the cliffs above you. Then you slowly turned
And gazed at me, your face-veil dropped at last,
Your lovely face lace-edged as by mantilla,
Your eyes burning with a blue diamond light.
Be not despondent, you said, all will be well.
Give me a broadsword, or a spear that I can wield.

Many weapons were swiftly held out to you.
You chose my sword, comrade of many battles.
What did you plan to do? To slaughter a victim?
Some human sacrifice, to bring down rain?
We waited, breathless and fearful.

                                        Again you eyed
Keenly the rock wall, seeming to us to pray.
Then, with strong, smooth steps, you swiftly climbed,
My sword in your hand, paused by a glittering slab.
You stroked it as a woman strokes a man,
Then, with a hawk's wild cry, you struck at it.
The blade did not shatter, but the slab was split,
Cracks spreading wide, like a starred window-glass.
Fragments shot out, the centre was spat forth.

Then came the water, rivulets, torrents, floods,
Splashing in cascades down the ravines.
A pond formed, a pool. We threw ourselves on it,
Circled like pilgrims round a sacred well.

We drank of your water, sweeter than man can say;
We raised grateful eyes to you, still high on the cliff.
Build here your home, you cried, around my spring!
Your sword, Captain; good fortune and farewell!
My blade flickered down like a lightning flash,
Pierced the impenetrable soil, stood quivering there.
Before our eyes, you shone, glimmered and faded,
Then vanished from sight, before we could shout our thanks.

My sword still stands erect on the spot where you flung it,
Its pommel fondled as a fertility charm,
Its hilt-bars handled as a source of hope,
Its blade, still sharp, grasped as a test of courage,
Its buried point the pledge of a journey ended.

Wiltshire,
February 1992.

CRATER LAKE

Crater, Athenian wine-cup, calm you lie,
Perfectly rounded, filled with deep blue sky.
Around your brim march palmtrees stark and still,
Their bright reflections bode not good but ill.
No wind or fish's fin ruffles this jewel,
But streams of bubbles hint at something cruel,
Some seething cauldron brewing devil's wine,
Far down, below your deepest sounding line.
Taste it - though fresh, its sulphur-tainted smell
Reeks of the banked-up furnaces of Hell.
What, with his spidery writing on the chart,
Meant that old Spanish captain to impart?
Ahi dracones: there be dragons here,
Lying in wait for mariners in this mere.
Within these blue unfathomable deeps,
A fire-and-brimstone-breathing monster sleeps.
Wake it not, reckless man, for soon or late,
Its lava will spew forth and seal your fate.

Grenada, Windward Islands,
July 1988.

13

OMENS: The Admiral and the Chickens

Preparing for action, on a brilliant day,
The warships trim, fast, with a crisp bow-wave,
This is my day, said the Admiral, I feel lucky,
To-day at last we shall crush the enemy.

But here comes the priest, the bloody augur,
Wheezily clambering up on to my poop,
With his absurd cageful of sacred chickens,
To rob me, the Admiral, of the decision
Whether to give battle to-day, or not.

Well, Publius, what have your wise fowls
To cluck to us to-day on strategy?

Legate, speak not so disrespectfully
Of the oracle, the gods' own messengers!
Here are the sacred birds, here the sacred grain.
You know the Reverend Flamen's ordinance:
Solemnly I, the gods' own harbinger,
Chanting holy prayers, shall duly scatter
This grain into their cage.
                              If they eat and dance,
We fight: if they abstain, we must withdraw.

I turn away, sickened by superstition.
Must a modern Admiral stomach such a farce?
I hear the old man's sacred invocation,
Allegedly chanted in the Etruscan tongue,
A secret language known only to priests.
I had better watch: or he'll report me
For sacrilege and gross neglect of duty.

There is the grain, lying spurned, uneaten,
Scattered, unwanted, on the cage's floor.
There are the accursed chickens squatting,
As if already sated, their martial ardour abated.
Not a nibble, not a dance among them:
(A prudent man would have had them starved before).

You see, Legate, the chickens do not eat,
Nor do they dance. So we do not fight.

I have the Carthaginians on my lee,
They are trapped downwind of us by reefs and shoals,
Hidden and treacherous, my foes' sure graveyard.
This could be the sea-fight to end the war.
If they will neither eat nor dance, I shout,
At least they shall drink!

I throw the cage down into the wine-dark sea,
And watch it sink to the last sacred bubble.
I order the captain:
                    Signal to the fleet,
We will engage the enemy at once!

As night falls, I withdraw my shattered remnants.
The fleet that once I felt so proudly mine
Is no man's any more. The chickens' will
Is the gods' will. They got the strategy right:
Not I.
          The dreadful fowls demand a sacrifice:
In the twilight of the battle, I fall upon my sword.

London; Wiltshire.
June 1992, October 1997.

15

FARANDOLE

Love is a dance,
A Farandole setting the heart on fire,
There is an Introduction, born of chance,
Full of sharp furious sound
And clash of brazen cymbals as the pair advance,
That often would the dancers fain retire,
Fearing a wound.

Fear not. The music moves into Adagio:
Here is deep exploration of sweet themes,
With softer interchange of moods and dreams,
While a great harmony,
A dawning symphony,
Builds up from muted voices Con corragio.

Now, minstrel, play your Minuet.
There is a need of contrapuntal art
To blend one yearning heart to another's heart.
Here they are met,
Set to a music formal still in note,
Yet they dance not by rote,
But terrible in their pride,
Like steeds curvetting fiercely under rein,
The blood in each hot vein
Strives to reveal what doubting heart would hide.
Play, minstrel, faster yet,
For they are come to the Allegro part.

<u>Allegro</u>, <u>Allegria</u>, joy divine!
Love needs no rein,
And no formality of mine and thine
Should still restrain
The perfect blending of these happy twain.
Play faster! Play more ardently! Oh, play!
The dancers their last figure have begun:
From eye to eye now glances love's bright ray,
The flames of their desire
Beat round them in an <u>Arabesque</u> of fire,
Fusing their flesh in one.

<u>Finale con fuoco</u>. Let it loudly peal!
For they, joined hand to hand and lip to lip,
Their garments, lovers' barriers, let slip,
A kiss to seal.
They pledge their bodies to each other's joy.
Nor time's slow-turning wheel
Shall quite destroy
The echoes of these solemn passion chords.

How ends their dancing? Tongue can shape no words.
No movement more entrancing
Than pirouette of painted humming-birds.
No music of the spheres
Can half depict the glory and the grace,
With which their naked beauties now embrace
The joy, the pain, the laughter and the tears.
Rapt in a vision splendid,
Their dance of love is ended.

Poona, India
March 1943

17

FIRST LUSTS

First the burning glance,
  And then our red corpuscles start to dance.
First the hand-in-hand,
  And then our senses no longer under command.
First the soft lips,
  And then the sinuous sarabande of the hips.
First the cool mouth,
  And then the torrid breezes of the south.
First the caress,
  And then the tender shedding of the dress.
First the breast,
  And then the sweet surrender of the rest.
First the gentle stroke,
  And then the flowering, towering, of the oak.
First the skin,
  And then within, within!
First the proud thrusts,
  And then the deep transcendence of our lusts.
First the exultant cry,
  And then the wave runs back, sigh after shuddering sigh.
First the carnal prod,
  And then the glimpse of God.

London,
May 1986.

BLACKBIRD LOVE

High up, among the treetops, we embrace,
Listening to the dawn blackbird.
His crystal notes resound in the growing light,
His music plays around our bodies,
Orchestrating our passions.

The bird proclaims:
                    This is my kingdom:
These are my boughs that I sing to defend,
Where we shall lay our eggs.
When you have flown away, and your nest is empty,
We shall still be here,
Singing, claiming our trees.

London,
May 1986.

MIDNIGHT VOYAGE

In the middle of the night,
Love rose softly, silently,
Lapping about our limbs,
Tide running strongly in the sea of dark,
Floating our sleeping bodies clear of the sand,
Rising and falling obedient to each wave's will,
Sliding into the off-shore current,
Outward bound.

On this midnight voyage,
Touch must be our pilot,
Kisses our compasses,
Flesh our destination,
As we set sail for ports and happy havens.

Here is the rudder, here the keel,
Step the mast, feel the wind's strong tug at the sheet,
Pierce the rising wave, dive into its trough.
Every wave whispers Now! breaking over us,
Now! and Now! and Now! is our master,
Oh, the wordless Now! murmured between our bodies,
Oh, the endless Now! singing within our souls.

Now the tall wave breaks on the harbour bar.
Now comes the lightning flash and the thunderbolt.
NOW! and again NOW!
The turbulent sea crashes around us.
We sink, we swim, we frolic in passion's waters.
And a last Now!

The sea subsides into smooth wavelets; the sand
Embraces our bodies once more in the sleep of love,
Caressed by ripples of the falling tide.
Peace and the dark descend round our bed again.
Our midnight voyage
Is accomplished.

Wiltshire,
May 1987.

LOVER'S LANDFALL

I am not alone, not one person but two.
What though Death with its methodical shears
Prunes my life-stem step by step,
Stripping the side-shoots of my kinship,
The foliage of my friends and peers.
I am not alone, nor cowed by fears,
    Having you.

I feel your aircraft's beat, its searchlight beam
Focuses on our bed, on which I lie,
Cleaving the sunrise in an earlier sky,
Bringing you home.
Are you asleep, dreaming of us and Rome?
You too are not alone, I am in your dream,
    Guarding you.

Here I rest in the warm Italian half-light,
Cradled in its pre-dawn silence,
Tracing the crystal rivulets of dew,
Watching for the sun, like a dolphin, golden bright,
To break surface out of the sea of night,
Scattering flames and phosphorescence,
Here I lie in radiant acquiescence,
    Waiting for day, and you.

Aeroporto Leonardo da Vinci, Rome,
June 1987.

HOUSE OF LOVE

This is the house of the heart,
Twin hearts with a single beat,
The house of understanding, all differences apart,
Where two minds meet;
The house of togetherness, with joint creations,
Where even trees and shrubs take up their stations,
By a single voice of command;
Where the flowers bloom on a jointly-fertile bush,
And the colours of life are mixed by a single hand,
On one palette, wielding a single brush.
As a chord of music sings
With a deeper and richer tone,
Different from the notes from which it springs;
As two trees entwine,
Seeking their sap and heartwood to combine,
And the graft taking, all other boughs forsaking,
The two woods are wedded together in one;
And their single stem bears, as its brilliant fruit,
The best qualities that each can contribute,
So we two are grafted, divinely crafted,
Into this house of love.

Wiltshire,
June 1989

REFUGE

This is the place of healing, the cone of silence,
Where the world's hates and griefs
Are stilled,
Where warm brickwork, cool rooms, glowing pictures,
Wide beds and amplest of kitchens,
Work on the soul.
This is a healing well.

This is the flower garden,
Bedded with deep rich soil,
Where grow not only fruit and flowers,
But ideas, too.
Here, thinking puts out roots,
Scatters pollen,
Thought-seed for the greenhouse of the mind.

This is the lambing fold. This house we made
Is loud with the calls of children
And their laughter,
Chasing each other through the rooms and the courtyard,
Like swallows and housemartins
Hawking for insects for their chicks.
This is a children's nest.

Nairobi and Kampala,
July 1992.

GARDENING IN THE THIRD AGE

I cultivate my sunset garden,
No vale of tears but a bowl of light,
Bidding my arteries not to harden,
Pruning back the growth of night.

Death, my not unfriendly neighbour,
Leaning over the garden wall,
Weighing up each daily labour,
Keeps himself within easy call.

With prudent effort, untaxed muscle,
I dig my tilth with mind and hand,
Fencing out life's din and bustle,
Letting others plough the sand.

As with Joshua, God suspending
The ruthless running of the sun,
Growth in this garden is not ending:
Planting has only just begun.

Wiltshire,
February 1988.

24

COMING HOME

I go out of the door of my old self,
I latch it behind me.
I venture into the darkness, my staff of trust
Clutched in my hand. I tread uncertainly,
Knowing not where I am bound, but quitting I was.
Ahead of me in the night are flickering flames,
Like will o' the wisp lights over treacherous marsh.
Am I fated to sink in that marsh?   But I must go forward.

I hear the river's music as I reach its bank,
Loud as a mountain burn running fast beneath ferns,
But dark and misty, stretching far ahead.
This is the river of my tears, my doubts, my fears,
This river I must cross to discover myself.
I pause above the fast stream. Will I drown in it?
No man drowns, they told me, in his own tears;
Take the plunge and strike out boldly - you will not sink.

I am naked, having stripped off the clothes of I was.
I dive in, I who never dived in my life.
I sink to the bottom, but swiftly rise to the top,
My tears bear me up, more buoyant than saltiest sea.
But my tears are bitter, saltier than that sea,
Burning my eyes, my lungs, my heart, like fire,
As they wash over my face, my lips, as I swim.
But as I taste and drink from the crest of each wave,
They begin to turn, drop by drop, into milk.
What wonderful sweetness of my erstwhile tears!

I swim faster, I leap as a dolphin leaps,
I glide like a flying fish, I skim through the air,
Bouncing from wavetop to wavetop like smooth-flung stone.
I touch ground underfoot. Is this the other shore?
Or can this be an island? But which? And whose?
I knew of no island out there when I took the plunge.

I rise from my tears, all naked and gleaming,
And run for the beach.
I glow in the dark, like fire reflected from sea,
The bright spray flashing about me, luminous green.
Surely I know this beach?
It is that beach! My beach!
Where the sand under my feet and between my toes
Is smooth as silk, but blazes like diamond dust,
With the palm-fronds' moon-cast shadows slatting the path
That leads over the turf to the trees beyond.
But the turf on to which I step from the sand is not grass,
But peacock feathers, smooth-laid, swathe upon swathe,
Soft underfoot, soft as my lover's skin,
And shining like dusky jewels in the dark.
And I suddenly know that the flames I saw from afar,
And took to be will o' the wisps floating on marsh
Were the fiery blooms of the peacock lawns I tread;
And the tears on my skin turn to pearls,
My sighs to laughter.
For now, at last, I perceive where I have come.
I am home, more home than ever I dreamed I could be.
This beautiful island is me:

Home is <u>I am</u>.

Nairobi,
September-October 1989.

APPLES OF MARBORK

The trees in this Polish forest
Are mostly young.
The ancient ones that dominated this landscape
Were shattered in battle,
Or heated the cooking-pots of so many soldiers
Of so many armies.   Over these wide plains
The fighting surged back and forth:
Steep tides in an estuary,
Smoothing the sands,
Leaving scarcely a seawrack behind.
But the trees are recolonising the wastelands.

Those in this country,
Now men and women of moment,
Were children then.
"In that building over there",
Remarks the Poznan physician,
"We hid in the basement while battle raged above us:
I was ten.   We were there for three weeks,
Never knowing our fate.   My uncle, you know,
A scoutmaster, aged twenty-one, was executed,
A victim, you could say, of lethal mis-translation,
Scouting to them meant spying."

Those who were older then, and are still alive,
Passed through grimmer purgatories.
"I was seventeen", says Alina, now seventy-three,
And dying in the hospice,
"When they took me away from Vilnius
To Vorkuta.
There was no food, no light,
It was very cold and very dark,
We hardly knew if we still existed".

Many survived out of these indomitable people,
But their faces are rugged,
Like trench-pitted landscapes,
Before the grass returns to soften them.
But neither trees nor grass can soften or blur
The oppressors' dreadful legacies,
Still scarring these human fields.

Along these dead-straight soldiers' roads,
Leading to Marbork, grim Teutonic fortress,
Once the channels of irresistible conquest,
There shine through the autumn mists
Baskets, bushels, of apples, red like roses,
Checking the wayfarer, tempting him to stop.
Apples of Poland, apples of Eden,
God's gift, first fruits of the newborn Earth,
Divine harvest of the tree of knowledge.
Sink your teeth deeply in their sweetness:
Poland lives.

Marbork, Poland,
May 1995.

COMFORT THE DYING

People dying of cancer - so many roads to death:
Terminal cases, when doctors can do no more.
What awaits the fading body, the uncertain soul?
Which of us lightly lifts his foot to that threshold,
Facing the infinite, unsure of immortality,
Wanting, as each of us does, "to make a good death."

What can "a good death" mean? Can earthly extinction
Be a good thing for man? Do we fear pain will betray us?
Pride in our deaths can only be tested by dying:
Too late then to adjust our stoic postures.
What can the stoic himself bear? Can he cross unflinching
That obscure frontier into the dark - or the light?

Doctors, nurses, set the scene, practise their arts.
They must suppress the pain, without drowning the mind.
Can we preserve our dignity, losing all else?
Let it be a man, not a beast, that sheds this life-skin.

Reply not with lies, but with truth, to our solemn questions:
Is this the end? And when and how shall we meet it?
Optimism and smiles, the evading half-truth,
Scarcely deceive the ear that now listens afar,
Are transparent to the eye that soon must close.
Does it matter whether the God who awaits us is real,
Or whether He is but the fiction of our hopes?
That which surely awaits us is real: the decay of flesh.

We must be brave and sane, if we are to swim
That Rubicon that bounds the realms of living.
We must build an earthly hospice to shelter us,
To teach and train us for that final leap
Into a void whose darkness for us shall be light.

Athletes are we, leaping for the highest bar,
Give us the pole, your staff of wisdom, to stay us.
Hospitallers, cheer us, catch us, cushion our fall,
Buoy us with truth. Let the warm wind of love
Bear us up, make of our drooping bodies a sail,
Billowing out as the white wave creams at the bow,
Bearing us God-knows-whither, but we no longer fear.

At Gostin's ancient monastery of Mary,
Our Blessed Lady of the Mystic Rose,
With its great dome pulsating with love and prayer,
Radiating to the world, so death-beset.
Here we exchange our wisdoms, strengthen our resolves.
Let the beacon that burns on the peak of this holy mountain
Be a lighthouse to men, illumine the reefs of death.
May our charts guide us, and our fellow-mariners,
To a haven no longer feared, but greeted with love.
Let there be wise men, wise women around us,
Let there be clear-eyed joy, not a wasted moment,
Squeezing each minute dry of its precious life-juice.

So let them say of our endings: This was no faintheart soul.
Never so lived he his life, as he lived his death.

Swieta Gora,
Gostin, Poland,
November 1988.

BREATH OF THE FOREST

The children of Poland,
After a death and the funeral,
Go into the forest to grieve.

The forest is all-encompassing,
Like a womb,
All of a greenness, green light, shadow, shade,

Fading, dying, decaying, growing
Being reborn.
And at its heart, it breathes,

Transpiring through its leaves
A solace to the spirit. This the children know;
They deeply inhale

The breath of the forest, draw deep breaths
Of easement. They can go home,
Begin their lives again.

Puszczykowo, Poland,
May 1997.

31

NIGHTINGALE AT SCUTARI: THOUGHTS OF AN <u>AMNESTY INTERNATIONAL</u> OBSERVER

On that cold day, I sat at Scutari, waiting
In that grim historic Turkish citadel,
Where Florence Nightingale had worked her miracles;
The young officers had shown me her quarters,
Preserved like a shrine, with many of her things.

And I waited at Scutari, pondering
How their heroine might have tackled my mission:
Political prisoners tortured, treated far worse
Than her own wounded soldiers, bearing worse scars,
Suffering nights of torment without respite.

And I waited, at Scutari, chilled, and seeking
Strength from that indomitable woman,
Who shamed those callous British generals,
Proclaiming to all the misery of war,
Nursing to health lives they had cast aside.

And I waited at Scutari, inwardly raging
At the brutal arrogance of soldiers
Wielding the powers of life and death and pain
Over defenceless human beings,
Claiming not to be accountable.

Then, at last, I stood up, at Scutari, reaching
For pen and paper.   In anger, but calmly,
I polished my most correct offensive French,
The language I shared with the Minister of Justice,
And with the torturers who disobeyed him.

And I couched my pen like a Crusader's lance, aiming
At His Excellency, the Turkish Army Commander:
Do you dare, I wrote, to obstruct us and our mission:
The right to see prisoners granted by your Government,
The duty of the world to champion the weak.

But the insolent Colonel at Scutari, smiling,
Said: We take no account of civilian ministers.
These are military matters.
                              But still, I said,
Take this letter to your Most Excellent General,
Don't try to suppress it: there is a copy.

Amnesty, which sent me to Scutari,
Shall see it, and his answer, if he makes one.
So we turned our backs upon Scutari, braving
Their anger, feeling naked between our shoulder blades.

But, in the end, we saw one prisoner.

Wiltshire,
September 1993.

DIALOGUE WITH TORTURERS: FURTHER THOUGHTS OF AN AMNESTY INTERNATIONAL OBSERVER.

Excellence vous attend, Maitre, suivez-moi.
I follow the flunkey, polishing my French.
Why French, I ask, in Turkey?   *Ah, monsieur,*
We old ones in Eastern Europe, Asia, we still speak
The tongue of diplomats, of civilised men.

Civilised? I ask myself, the tongue of torturers?
Do I know enough of their vocabulary?
Should I have brought a torturers' dictionary?

Excellence, je me presente, avocat anglais,
Rapporteur international pour Amnesty.

The Minister's lip curls: *Bienvenu, friend of assassins.*
You come to beg mercy for those who show it not.

Excellency, reflect, are we not all human?
Is not frail flesh too vulnerable, not lawful prey
For the lusts, the cruelties of any gaoler?
Which of us is safe from the sadist's lash?

Appellez-vous ces animaux humains?
Their wickedness forfeits your pacific claims.
Rebellious spirits must yield their bodies up
To the power of the State, the need that truth be told.

Will you not, sir, concede this point at least,
That those whom you torture tell the truth they know?
Your extorted truth for them would be a lie:
They are driven to perjury to abate their pain.

Parbleu, c'est formidable, your mission here!
British hypocrite, know you not Ulster's gaols,
Full of brave spirits, challenging your yoke?
Shine your brave torch into torture chambers there!

I have here, sir, our own Judges' report
Upon the prisons you speak of. Would you not wish
To be exonerated, too?
                      What, yield up sovereignty
To our alien enemies, plotting our downfall?

Is this your last word, Minister: of hate?
Do you wish to be immortalised by such phrases?
What harm can it do for me to see the prisoners?
If all is well, my report will clear your name.

The Minister ponders.   Pawn of the General Staff,
Dare he open their prison doors to me?
But still, the publicity could profit him,
His Government needs some praise, to offset the blame.

Very well, Maitre, you shall see a prisoner.
One only, mind; you must make do with her,
Tomorrow at the prison, at nine precisely.
Do not be late: this is your only chance.

So I am to see a female prisoner:
Could she be the wife of the chief accused,
A medical student, a girl of good family,
One of Grahame Greene's "untorturables"?

We gather at Scutari, cold grim fortress,
The Procureur-General is there, the Governor too,
Neither official speaking any English.
With my interpreter I command the field.
The prisoner - still just a girl - suddenly enters,
Raven-haired, bright-eyed, pale, prison-garbed,
And speaking English! I explain our role;
Their affidavits have told me what to ask.

My guess was right: she is an "untorturable".
At least so far - but not so for her husband,
Nor all the others of whom I have the names.
We interpret to the officials what she says,
But they seem not to care. What do they think?
The prisoner deals with the torturers' technology,
The Turkish bastinado which they use
For beating prisoners on the soles of their feet.

She draws its picture for me, a shape I know.
What will the Governor think of this disclosure?
He does not object, she signs the sketch, I sign it,
The Procureur-General, the Governor, also sign.
The Lord hath delivered them into our hands.
The Council of Europe will have plenty to bite on.
Signed, sealed, settled. The prisoner bids farewell.

Peace, I say to myself. the charm's wound up.

Ankara and Istanbul,
February - August 1972

Note: The report by Amnesty International to the
Council of Europe on this mission led to an improvement
in the treatment of prisoners in Turkey.

SNOWBIRDS

The gulls roost in the leafless tree like snowballs
Thrown by children, caught in a cage of twigs.
To warm themselves, they ruffle up their feathers,
Their snowy stillness gleams in the winter sky.

Heart reaches up to touch that gleaming stillness,
To share their white uncomplicated peace,
To warm itself at their soft-feathered heartbeats,
To drown itself in their deep lustrous eyes.

A distant shot explodes my feathered lanterns,
Dissolving them in a snow-storm of alarm,
Leaving my tree naked, and me in mourning
For the loss of our magic moment out of time.

Wiltshire,
May 1988.

STOURHEAD

The sky is the colour of an oyster-shell,
Which the lake reflects,
Rippled by the diligent aimless patterns of the ducks.
The ancient trees that it mirrors
Are only three times older than me.
The bridge's dimming arches
Are eyes looking up at me, watching,
Counting my minutes.
The calls of my grandchildren, returning,
Tell me that this precious day
Is reaching its end,
In my still intermittent dusk.

Stourhead, Wiltshire.
December 1992.

DARK LADY: ON FINDING AN OLD POEM

Could the writer of this have been me?
Could this Dark Lady have been she?
Let me borrow his lips, his pen,
Deck her in the Dark Lady's gown, and then
Enjoy again her prized virginity.

Alcudia, Mallorca,
February 1992.

THE SLEEPING FOOL: Looking at a painting by
Cecil Collins, 1943.

Here I sit, fretted by waiting
To be made to laugh,
Waiting with jaws agape, muscles aching
With the need for a psychic release by mirth.
There lies our Fool, with a degree in Folly,
A Master's in manic metaphor,
Appointed Jester-in-Chief by the King my husband,
With a generous stipend.
There he sleeps like a log, heedless of us,
His legs crossed like a Crusader's effigy,
Clutching firmly his mad cap of office,
As the wind drones through the trees,
Straining the blossoms.
So he cannot, in fact, be quite unconscious.
How can we and our court survive, stay sane,
Be liberated from the deadly feudal tedium,
Without our daily dose of drollery?
Wake him, my ladies, we have a need to laugh.

Dorset,
1996.

WHAT I AM NOW

What I am now
Is not what I was;
But what I was
Is part of what I am now.
For what I was
Is the history of what I am,
Seen through the backward vision of myself,
Scenery which recedes from me
As in a train,
Eclipsed by the first tunnel it encounters.
But on this train of myself
I have as companions
Those who were with me,
But were not of me.
Changed now, they too
Are part of what I am.

Nairobi,
October 1989.

REASON TO BELIEVE

What have I got good reason to believe?
What has anyone got? Does the policeman
Have reason to believe a man is drunk,
As I have reason, or am supposed to have,
To believe that there really is a God?

Have I reason to believe that I am good,
And others are evil? What infallible signs
Tell us what we know not, but must surmise?
Are there things totally unbelievable?

Thomas would not believe Jesus was risen,
Not even with putting his fingers in the wounds:
"Doubting Thomas" for ever condemned to be.
Stigmata are wounds, as real as Jesus' own,
Does the mind of him who bears them truly believe
That he is Jesus?
                    Credo quia impossibile,
Augustine said. Must belief be of the possible,
Or may it be of the impossible? Can a man
Die, but truly die, and rise again?
Can a person be in two places at once?

Domestic apparitions can perform
Such feats. The witness touched by the icy hand
Of what he would call a ghost sincerely believes
In what he felt, and solemnly would so swear.
Does he have reason to believe, more than the policeman,
Or less?
                    Out there, our eyes see stars by the billion,
Every millionth star a sun, they tell us,
With planets like ours. Do I believe, with reason
So to do, that out there a being like me
Is writing a poem, a mirror-image of mine?
How many suns do I need to believe in,
To be certain of the existence of other worlds?
Do their mortals, two-headed, six-legged or amphibians,
Have reason to believe in their own Saviour?

The unknowability of the Universe
May be my reason's true and best protection.
Have I not reason to believe, that I should not believe?

Wiltshire
August 1992.

PLANETARIUM

What will become of the pudding in my skull,
That giant walnut-kernel, soft yet crinkly,
Whose cortex-surface, rolled out flat, like pastry,
Would carpet a room? Inside its cool, grey jelly
Lie all the magic parts that make up I:
Cerebrum, cerebellum, thalamus,
Hypothalamus, pineal eye, the neurons
By the billion firing through their synapses,
Each thought of mine flashed by their lightning transits,
Expressed in chemical language unimaginable.

The I which is me sits in my planetarium,
Watching my million million constellations,
The myriad stars ablaze in my private universe.
Neurons streak like shooting stars as I think.
Each mind-country has its own star-cluster.
Here is love, here sorrow, joy, anxiety,
Here poetry, brilliant ideas, superb inventions,
Here are my memories, dense like galaxies.
The book I have read, the book I shall write tomorrow,
Stand ready stored in the library in my head.

How can it die, my universe, tiny yet huge,
How does it learn its last synapse has fired?
It must know about dying: a knowledge programmed
In every thinking, hoping, wondering part.
Most mortals anticipate, seek to combat, death,
With an ultimate blast of energy from the depths,
That makes the dying revive, bestow last blessings:
Some high intelligence sensing the end is nigh.
What is it that, in advance, measures my life-span,
Rolls back the shadows for a final stand?

What will then become of my planetarium?
Can a mystical universe brusquely be dissolved
Into mere clay or ashes? Surely some element
Flies on beyond our own short ration of life,
On which such eternal magic would be wasted.
Horace the poet, the Emperor Hadrian, asked,
"Shall I totally die, will not some part of me,
Some tiny, timid, wandering soul, survive?"
Computer folk put machine-data on disk:
Is there a disk to store the bytes of me?

Flash on, bright stars, speed through your synapses,
Make your junctions as fast as light can shine,
Connect one sight, one thought, at once with another,
Writing your own scenario as you go.
Forget me not, my neurons, fire on for ever,
In some other dimension you must know,
But I cannot imagine. So shall the I
That owns you, but whom you make up, live on.
Make some invisible galaxy your new home,
Flying my flag over my planetarium.

Nairobi,
October 1992.

THE GOD OF THE GALAXIES

The crowded transepts of the Abbey shake
To the thunder of a thousand youthful voices,
Glorifying God and rejecting Satan,
Affirming the existence of a happy Hereafter.
They are not deceived, these youthful souls,
Proclaiming the existence of their God,
God, whatever God is, from their birth painted
Within their minds a picture of Himself,
Which their souls, which all we humans need,
To make this world a place we can accept.
This God of all galaxies, of all dimensions,
Presents Godness in the vernacular
To every creature who needs It to exist.

Out beyond the blue sky, into the dark
In which all creation is forever wrapped,
Pierced only by immensely distant stars,
Lit only by the flames of nebulae,
Out beyond the uttermost galaxy,
Something is there, Something created us.
Must we not all adore our own First Cause,
Just as much as Its local embodiment,
As much as Jesus, Mahomet, Brahma, Buddha?

Are they not all Gods, each and every one,
Tending the needs and hopes of all mankind?
They are the shadows thrown by the flickering fire
Upon the rough rock walls of Plato's cave,
Shadows of the True, of the Ideal,
Seen by each man, each woman, in their own guises,
In a universe otherwise void and without meaning.

God is every god, all gods are God,
Wherever the breath of consciousness has tamed
The brute within these lumps of clay, ourselves.
The line of Gods extends like stepping-stones
Across the river of the universe.
Mankind steps from one stone to another,
Rising higher - if higher it is - with every step.

Sometimes we stumble, or we slip and fall,
Sometimes we are knocked off by rival zealots,
Sometimes stepping back to the warmth we know,
Recoiling from the Unknown: but mostly onwards.
Whither will our Godly stepping-stones lead us?
Does our First Cause recede, as we advance
Towards the Knowledge - a cosmic will-o-the-wisp?

The Tree of Knowledge in our Garden of Eden
Must have been a reflection
Of the unattainability of the Ideal.
No wonder Jehovah was so sad, so angry,
At Adam and Eve's partaking of that fruit.
Not to be punished were they cast out of Eden,
But to live in Shadowlands, their souls protected
From the lethal radiance of omniscience.

To know all, but really all, to enter
Into the very mind of God, to be absorbed
Into Its absolutes: who would wish it?
Not for nothing has the Black Hole become
A bogey for the astronomers, the space-men.
Infinite gravitation, infinite force:
To have all knowledge, maybe, is to have nothing.

Westminster Abbey, London,
December 1992.

47

TIME-STEALER

The drops of my life slide through your narrow sluice;
Water, not sand, is the measuring rod I watch.
The Greeks had a word for you: Klepsydra,
Water-stealer, drip by drip, like a clock's tick,
Calibrated by sun and the gnomon's shadow,
Time-keeper, master of hours-flow. Long-winded
Greek orators were ruled by you, in bitter debate,
Challenging their opponents to reply: _In my water._

Time-stealer, bleeding away my seconds,
How can you steal my time, not mine to be stolen?
It was not your own hand that filled my flask,
Or shrank or stretched your neck to beat my tempo,
Orifice, gateway, bottleneck, needle's eye,
Through which the destined steps of all mankind
Must pass, be they rich or poor, happy or sad,
Each englobed in his drop, like sperms in semen.

Hour-glass, life-glass, hope-glass,
The iridescent walls of your upper sphere
Reflect the tints of the days that you have counted:
Days when your flow seems frozen, halcyon days,
Days when it rushed by, days too rashly spent,
Days, hours, minutes, seconds, before departures,
Millenia embraced in a welcoming kiss.

Drops of history, drops of love and affliction,
Drops flowing over as from that porphyry font,
By which we dallied in magic Tuscan gardens.
Drip, drip, Palladio, you will live for ever,
So long as the fish have water and lilies bloom.
Time-stealer, take me swimming in your own water,
You've drained my glass. Look seaward, my tide's run out.

London,
November 1991.

48

JESSES

The planet spins, and spins away my life,
Spooling me up at one end, tailing off at the other,
Watched by the Fates, those spinsters three,
Lachesis, Clotho and Atropos,
Poised over me with their implacable shears.
Why should these women spin away man's life?
Does the giver of life have a right to fix its term,
Some mortal privilege won by their wombs' birth-gift?

One holds one's children by such silken threads,
Too fierce a tug, and off the bird is flown,
Free - like a falcon soaring aloft with its jesses,
Free - to be lost, shot down, starved out, ensnared.
A man's life hangs upon a thread no stronger.
Tugging at your fate may seal your end,
But less need then for snipping by those dread scissors.

Oh, snip my thread, unleash my jesses too.
Or, if you will not,
Let me, let me tug myself!
Let the long pull,
And the strong pull,
And the last pull,
Be mine!

Wiltshire,
December 1990.

49

ROAD TO THE PASS

Ten years are not too long,
To marshal the memories that throng
The long tree-lined avenue of our life together.
Our memories cheer us, wave their banners, prance,
Blow their trumpets, clash their cymbals, dance,
Point happily, proudly, to the statues,
To the monuments, the inscriptions, the memorial trees,
That line the route that we have trod so far,
Recording all we have done and they remember.
We wave back, blow kisses, call out to each their name.
They are our children, fruit of our thoughts,
Tokens of fame,
Harvest of our labours,
Of our risks and our adventures.

The road along which they march towards us,
Stretching back so far,
Goes on behind us around the corner out of sight,
Towards a blue horizon.
A notch in the distant hills
Marks the high pass that leads to that other country,
Towards which we shall be trekking on from here.
The landscape in between us and the pass
Is closely wooded, allowing no distant views.
The way through it is unmapped, unpredictable.
But the forest paths, no matter how dark and deep,
Shall not deter us, nor give us pause,
Nor sow any doubt or despondency in our hearts.
Like Robert Frost's horseman,
Waiting, listening in the snow,
We have promises to keep,
And miles to go before we sleep,
For ever,
Together.

Wiltshire.
4 July 1996.

CONDUCTED TO EARTH

Be not distressed, my darling, if my poems
Treat of mortality, the death of flesh.
They are but age's cunning stratagems
To keep the unconquerable spirit fresh.

Age cannot help but breed such thoughts within,
Like powerful electric charges they build,
Coursing remorselessly beneath my skin.
They need to be earthed, their lethal forces stilled.

Each such poem I write is a little death,
A sacrifice to defer the ultimate doom
That lies in wait for every living breath,
Watching the calendar leaves in a lonely room.

Thus my mournful poems are the basis,
Not for catalysis but for catharsis.

Nairobi,
October 1992.

51

HERACLITUS IS DEAD

Today, in town, I heard a merchant say:
"Heraclitus is dead, in some far away
City, Halicarnassus it could be."
Far away from here, not far from me:
Our friendship was always as close as night to day.
My eyes poured libations for your obsequies,
Mourning that never more, in festive array,
Shall we two recite, in the dusk above the bay.
But my tears mingle with my memories
Of your nightingale's voice singing the sun to sleep;
Though your body now is buried fathoms-deep,
Death shall not steal your music with your clay.

After Simonides.

Wiltshire,
August 1992

THIS SIDE OF THE HILL

When I am no longer here,
Think of me as I once was or would have been.
When I am not here,
I am still there, or in the in-between.
When I am no longer here,
Let yourself be not here either.
You must be where I was, and shall be then.
Ask yourself not the why or the when
That I departed, but from whence, to go thither.
Take up Time's pen,
Trace back along the calendar's path,
Time-travel with me and to me, who was and am still
This side, not the other side of the hill,
Smiling at you, across our bright brave hearth.

Wiltshire,
February 1991.

THE GRAIN OF MY LIFE

How many years have I basked under the sky,
How many years weathered under the rain and wind?
Good years and bad, fat years and thin,
Each year investing my flesh with its gossamer skin,
Building up, layer by layer, my mortal rind,
All of them making up the man that is I.

This trunk of mine is my life's timber-store:
In serried rows the year-long standards lie,
Clear-felled by time's relentless knife,
Marshalled by decades since my first birth-cry.
Each timber tongue speaks with the sap of its year:
Their tones and textures chart the grain of my life.

Wickerwork years, cradling earliest thoughts;
Years of the pine, the bright-scrubbed nursery table;
Sycamore years, dancing, prettily patterned;
Years of the chestnut - shining conker matches;
Willow years, of the deep-oiled cricket bat;
Years of rosewood, inlaid with lovers' knots;
Matchwood years, splintered by war and loss;
Years of the smooth-cheeked walnut rifle stock;
Sandalwood years, trapped in the perfumed east;
Years of oak, robust with work and achievement;
Mahogany years, richly reflecting candles;
Years of the elm-plank, coffining deaths of dear ones;
Satinwood years, deeply bloomed with love.
These have fashioned the marquetry of my days.

This trunk of mine itself is seed-sown timber,
Seed of my father, seedling, sapling, tree,
Spreading its branches widely, flowering free,
Lord of the forest, sheltering lives without number,
A county's landmark, tall over flowering meads.
One day the frost strikes, beetles bore, blight bleeds,
Wounding majesty, signing wood's death-warrant,
And the dying begins, leaf by dry leaf beneath.

Now comes the logger - "tree-surgeon" now his trade -
Ranging the forest with his saw, knight-errant,
Beating the coverts for trees that are blazed for death,
Like white-nosed chargers of a doomed brigade.
He makes the first cut, spurting mortal sawdust,
Then slices through deep layers of time long past.
The sawdust-spattered monarch, severed at last,
Sways, falls, faster, thrashing of leaves, a crash
That makes the earth leap; lopping of limbs, slash
Burned in the fire, eyes smarting, every heartstring
Tugged by the dead tree's ghostly fingering.
The great bole rolled away reveals a clearing,
Ash-carpeted, pink with sunlit fireweed, awash
With memories of a lost shadow, cool and vast.
So beaches the log of life, its grain stuck fast.

Look at this lonely tree-stump, polished, massive,
Closely whorled with the thumbprint of a life,
This children's picnic table, dumb and passive,
Primrose-girt and shaded by purple loosestrife,
This sylvan stage, from which the blackbird sings,
Once was a man. See, these are his rings.

Wiltshire,
1988-1991

MUIR HUNTER QC

Muir Hunter's poetry is the product of a long and distinguished public life. Educated at Westminster and Christ Church, Oxford - where he read Classics - he helped to evacuate children from republican Spain during the civil war. He served in Intelligence during the 2nd world war and since then has practised as a barrister and Queen's Counsel.

He writes the standard bankruptcy textbook, <u>Muir Hunter on Personal Insolvency</u>, and edits other legal works. He was the leading counsel in the sensational Poulson bankruptcy case; his determination to expose corruption in high places, in the teeth of establishment opposition, earned him the sobriquet "the British McCarthy" and the attentions of the international media. He is still invited to comment on the case and its contemporary implications.

Muir and his wife, Gillian Petrie, helped to establish Nairobi Hospice and founded Polish Hospices Fund. He has worked extensively as a lawyer in east Africa and as a legal observer of political trials in Africa and Turkey for <u>Amnesty International</u>. He founded Britain's first neighbourhood law centre and is a governor of the Royal Shakespeare Theatre. His poems arise from this rich mixture of experiences and his knowledge of the Classics and several European languages. Muir's poems about Poland have been translated into Polish and published there.

Muir comes from a well-known writing dynasty: his grandfather was Chief Editor of Reuter's, his uncle was the leading spy novelist of his time and his mother was a novelist. As a poet, Muir has kept his work secret until recent years when he began to publish, to great acclaim, in <u>Tears in the Fence</u> and the publications of East Street Poets.

Brian Hinton,
Associate Editor, TEARS IN THE FENCE.